Reptile Babies

Catherine Veitch

Heinemann
LIBRARY
Chicago, Illinois

Edited by Daniel Nunn, Rebecca Rissman,
and Catherine Veitch
Designed by Cynthia Della-Rovere
Picture research by Ruth Blair
Production by Victoria Fitzgerald
Originated by Capstone Global Library
Printed and bound in China by South China Printing
Company

Library of Congress Cataloging-in-Publication Data
Veitch, Catherine.
  Reptile babies / Catherine Veitch.
      p. cm.—(Animal babies)
  Includes bibliographical references and index.
  ISBN 978-1-4329-7496-1 (hb)
  ISBN 978-1-4329-8421-2 (pb)
  1. Reptiles—Infancy—Juvenile literature. I. Title.
QL644.2.V45 2014
  597.9139—dc23   2012033198

Acknowledgments
Getty Images: burcintuncer, back cover, 22 right, Frans
Lemmens, 7, Rich Carey, 22 left; Minden Pictures: Pete
Oxford, 12; Nature Picture Library: Anup Shah, 13, 17,
Barry Mansell, 6, George McCarthy, 15, Hanne & Jens
Eriksen, 11, Ingo Arndt, cover, 14, John Cancalosi,
20, Jurgen Freund, 18, Konstantin Mikhailov, 19, 23
bottom, Nature Production, 8, Tony Phelps, 21, 23 top,
16; Science Source: Jim Merli, 9; Shutterstock: Evgeny
Murtola, 1, 4, idreamphoto, 2, 5 bottom left, Monica
Cristale, 5 top right, Paul Tessier, 10 bottom right, paytai,
5 top left, Pongphan.R, 22 top, RUDVI, 5 bottom right,
23 middle

We would like to thank Michael Bright for his invaluable
help in the preparation of this book.

Every effort has been made to contact copyright holders
of material reproduced in this book. Any omissions will
be rectified in subsequent printings if notice is given to
the publisher.

Contents

What Is a Reptile?

scales

Reptiles have scaly skin.

snake

lizard

turtle

crocodile

Snakes and lizards are reptiles.
Turtles and crocodiles are reptiles.

How Are Baby Reptiles Born?

eggs

Most reptiles lay eggs on land.

This turtle digs a hole in the sand.
She lays her eggs in the hole.

This snake digs a hole in the soil.
She lays her eggs in the soil.

babies

Some reptiles give birth to
live babies.

Caring for Eggs

Some reptiles look after their eggs until they hatch.

Many reptiles leave their eggs
in nests.

Hatching

Some reptiles break out of their eggs themselves.

Some reptile parents break the
shells of their babies' eggs.

Most reptile babies look like their parents.

This baby turtle looks like its parents.

Caring for Baby Reptiles

Some reptiles care for their babies.

baby

This crocodile carries her baby to a safe place.

Growing Up

Most baby reptiles look after themselves. They find a new home.

prey

They catch their own prey.

Baby reptiles grow bigger.
They hide from predators.

They find a new mate.

Life Cycle of a Reptile

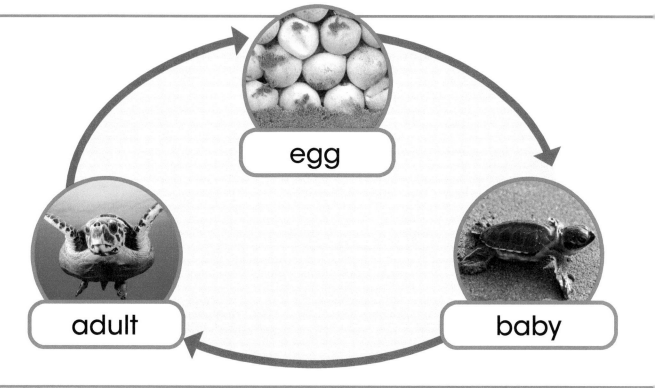

egg

adult

baby

A life cycle shows the different stages of an animal's life. This is the life cycle of a turtle.

Picture Glossary

 **mate** male or female that an animal has babies with

 **predator** animal that eats other animals

 **prey** animal that is eaten by other animals

Index

Notes to Parents and Teachers

Before reading

Show children a collection of photos and videos of reptiles. National Geographic and PBS are useful websites. Explain what a reptile is and discuss the characteristics of reptiles.

After reading

- Mount photos of adult and baby reptiles on note cards and play games of concentration where the children have to match a baby reptile with its parent. Model the correct pairs first.

- Ask children to label the parts of a reptile: for example, head, feet, tail, scales.

- Look at page 22 and discuss the life cycle stages of a reptile. Mount photos of the egg, baby, and adult stages and ask children to put the photos in order. Encourage children to draw a life cycle of a human to compare.

- Compare how different reptiles care for their babies. Discuss the care human babies need.

- To extend children's knowledge, the reptiles are as follows: gecko: p. 4; skink with eggs: p. 6; leatherback turtle: p. 7; tiger snake: p. 8; skink with young: p. 9; Burmese python: p. 10; green turtle: p. 11; tortoise hatching: p. 12; Nile crocodile: p. 13; chameleon adult and baby: p. 14; freshwater turtle adults and hatchling: p. 15; adder with baby: p. 16; Nile crocodile holding hatchling: p. 17; green turtle hatchlings: p. 18; hatchling grass snake: p. 19; spiny lizard: p. 20; adders courting: p. 21.